Learning to read. Reading to learn!

LEVEL ONE Sounding It Out Preschool–Kindergarten
For kids who know their alphabet and are starting to sound out words.

learning sight words • beginning reading • sounding out words

LEVEL TWO Reading with Help Preschool–Grade 1
For kids who know sight words and are learning to sound out new words.

expanding vocabulary • building confidence • sounding out bigger words

LEVEL THREE Independent Reading Grades 1–3
For kids who are beginning to read on their own.

introducing paragraphs • challenging vocabulary • reading for comprehension

LEVEL FOUR Chapters Grades 2–4
For confident readers who enjoy a mixture of images and story.

reading for learning • more complex content • feeding curiosity

Ripley Readers Designed to help kids build their reading skills and confidence at any level, this program offers a variety of fun, entertaining, and unbelievable topics to interest even the most reluctant readers. With stories and information that will spark their curiosity, each book will motivate them to start and keep reading.

RIPLEY PUBLISHING

Vice President, Licensing & Publishing Amanda Joiner
Editorial Manager Carrie Bolin

Editor Jessica Firpi
Writer Korynn Wible-Freels
Designer Mark Voss
Reprographics Bob Prohaska

Published by Ripley Publishing 2020

10 9 8 7 6 5 4 3 2 1

Copyright © 2020 Ripley Publishing

ISBN: 978-1-60991-342-7

For more information regarding permission, contact:
VP Licensing & Publishing
Ripley Entertainment Inc.
7576 Kingspointe Parkway, Suite 188
Orlando, Florida 32819

Email: publishing@ripleys.com
www.ripleys.com/books
Manufactured in China in January 2020.

First Printing

Library of Congress Control Number: 2019954289

PUBLISHER'S NOTE
While every effort has been made to verify the accuracy of the entries in this book, the Publisher cannot be held responsible for any errors contained in the work. They would be glad to receive any information from readers.

PHOTO CREDITS

Ripley Readers

Trains!

All true and unbelievable!

RIPLEY
PUBLISHING

a Jim Pattison Company

Have you ever been on a train?

Trains can carry
people and cargo.

Before trains, there were stagecoaches.

They had to stop for new horses so the old ones could rest.

It could take months to get somewhere on a stagecoach!

Trains help people get to places a lot faster.

The first train was slow.
A horse could outrun it!

There are a lot of ways
to make a train go.

Some use fire and water
to make steam.

Steam trains were
the first to carry
a lot of people.

There were a lot of
train tracks in 1916.

All of them could have reached the Moon!

Some steam engines burn coal.

We find coal deep
down in the ground.

Diesel trains are big and fast.

They can do more than
steam trains can.

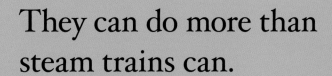

That electric train is
good for the earth.

It does not make black smoke.

Wow! A bullet train
can go really fast.

It can beat a racecar!

Look up! Some trains run over the city.

There are trains under the ground, too!

Would you like to
take a train ride up
in the mountains?

There are so many
cool kinds of trains!

LEVEL TWO · Reading with help

Ripley Readers

All true and unbelievable!

Ready for More?

Ripley Readers feature unbelievable but true facts and stories!

LEVEL ONE · Sounding it out

LEVEL TWO · Reading with help

LEVEL THREE · Independent reading

LEVEL FOUR · Chapters

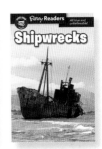

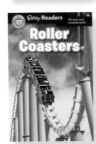
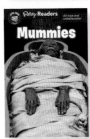

For more information about Ripley's Believe It or Not!, go to www.ripleys.com